Big Life Lessons
from
Nature's Little Secrets

A Nature Journal
for Kids

Pamela Baxter

BIG Life Lessons

from Nature's Little Secrets

A Nature Journal for Kids

PAMELA BAXTER

Hidden Oasis Publishing

Dedicated to my parents,
for sharing their love of nature with me—
on hikes and nature walks,
in backyard discoveries and experiments,
and with pencils and paints,
trying to capture the beauty of it all.

Also by Pamela Baxter

A Cup of Light
(published by Skinner House Books)

**Hidden Oasis
Publishing**
P.O. Box 80
Kimberton, PA 19442

Paperback ISBN 978-0-9884636-0-8
Library of Congress Control Number: 2017913145

Acknowledgements

This book represents the weaving together of so many threads of my life and the people in it, some of whom I never met but who left behind words and pictures that inspired and informed me. Thanks to all of them.

In the present, I want to thank the children who took an early version of my book for a "test drive" and filled out their evaluation forms so seriously: Aivre, Evan, Sydney, Hyacinth, Anna, Joshua, and Evelyn.

Thank you to all my friends who listened to my ideas and provided encouragement along the way—Marcia Tate, Diana Rebel, Barbara Robinson, Jennifer Feld, Rachel Lane, Heidi Frayer, Charmian Cutler, Cathy Vogt, Joe Poz, and Sarah Kotchian.

Also, thanks to Annette Murray at Sticky Earth Books for her expertise in design, layout, and publishing, and for her continuing enthusiasm for my project. And to Cindy Huffman, Ad Concepts and Copy, for her professional editing and proofreading.

Finally, thanks, to my partner, Charlie Crawford, for his unstinting, cheerful support, for reviewing my manuscript with his excellent English-teacher's eye, and for never doubting that I would get it done.

You are invited...

Step outside your door, and there's a big, wide world around you—the world of nature. The natural world provides everything you need: air to breathe, water to drink, and food to eat. It also supplies all the raw materials that people use to make other useful things: iron ore to make steel, oil to make plastic, plant fiber to make fabric and paper, ingredients to make medicines, plus all the things that go into cell phones, computers, light bulbs, and toothbrushes . . . the list is almost endless.

Yet nature does even more. If you know how to look and listen, you'll find that nature can also teach you many things. For instance, it can teach you how to

- be yourself
- do your best
- make good choices
- prepare for the future
- know when to stand strong and when to be flexible

That's what this book is about. It's a little peek into the natural world, exploring things that anyone can discover just by paying attention. Each section will help you see things you may never have noticed before—things that can help you be the best person you can be.

How to use this book

This is *your* book. Read it. Write in it. Use the blank pages in the back to draw on, and add pictures or photos. Find your own things in nature to wonder about and learn from. Even if you live in a city or a town, there are still plenty of places to explore, perhaps a tree on your block or a flower in a garden. Look up! Look down! Nature is all around.

Enjoy!

Table of Contents

1 Paying Attention

When I was out walking this morning, I saw a garden snake stretched out right in the middle of the road. The snake wasn't moving, so I thought it must be dead. But when I stepped a little closer, I saw the snake give a wriggle. It was definitely alive!

I feel sad when I see wildlife that's been squished by cars, and I didn't want this snake to get run over, too. But how could I get it out of the road without touching it? Even though garden snakes don't carry venom, they can still bite!

Hoping to scare the snake away, I moved closer so that I was at its tail end and started stamping my feet. Sure enough, the snake silently started to move in quick, graceful S-curves and disappeared off the road and into the grass. I realized that in scaring the snake, I saved it.

· · · ● · · · ● · ·. · ● · · ·

Sometimes, things in our lives can feel scary to us. That can actually be good! Scary things can make us sit up and take notice. They can help us stay safe.

Some things that are dangerous are easy to spot. We see a "Caution" sign and know that we need to stay away from something. We hear a car horn and we wait to cross the street. But some things that are dangerous are harder to see or hear. Sometimes the caution sign is in our body—an icky feeling in our stomach or prickles on the back of our neck.

Maybe a friend has asked us to do something we're not sure is right. Our heart might start to beat really fast, or we might feel like we just swallowed a rock. That's our body talking to us. It's saying, "This isn't right. Please don't do it!" If we're not sure how to say "no" to our friend, we can talk to our parents about it.

Maybe we're super-nervous about a test that's coming up. We get "butterflies" in our stomach and don't feel like eating. We can pay attention to that signal and study a little more or talk to our parents or our teacher about our anxiety. We can listen to a song that makes us feel happy. We can remember something that we did a really good job on.

What do YOU think?

What are some things that have scared you?

What did you do to stay safe or confident?

2 Observing

When there's fresh snow on the ground, I love to go outside and look for animal tracks in the yard. In the snow near the birdfeeder, I usually see the footprints of birds, squirrels, rabbits, and sometimes even deer.

One January morning after a snowstorm I found a paw print I'd never seen before. It was small, with five toes. What could it be? Curious, I followed the tracks across the snow-covered backyard, under the trees, back to where I'd started, and then all the way to the front yard. This animal was quite a wanderer!

I went inside to get a ruler so that I could measure the size of an individual print and the distance between two prints. Then I got out my animal identification book. What would the mystery animal turn out to be?

The prints with five toes measured about one inch by one inch, just the right size for a skunk. But there weren't any claw marks, and the walking pattern wasn't a match. No matter how hard I tried, I couldn't make a skunk fit the trail. I was stumped!

There was only one thing to do: check my first observations. I followed the trail of paw prints under the trees, crouched down, and took a closer look. Here, in the shade of the pine trees, the prints were protected from the warmth of the sun. Here, the prints looked a little different. They were more crisp and clear. Suddenly, I could see that the animal that had left the tracks had only four toes.

Four toes? I burst out laughing. The wild creature I was hoping to discover was my neighbor's cat!

· · · ● · · · ● · ▪ · ● · · ·

Many times, we think we see all there is to see, or we think we have all the facts about something. We all do this. But if what we believe disagrees with what a friend believes, we might get into an argument, with each of us insisting we're right. The problem is that when each of us is so sure we're right, we don't really listen to each other. Before we know it, we're fighting. We might even decide we're not friends anymore.

What do YOU think?

Have there been times when you've made a decision about something and then learned you didn't have all the facts?

What did it feel like to accept the new information?

How hard was it to change your mind?

3 Belonging

Look up in the sky, and what might you see? If you're lucky, along with a beautiful blue sky you'll also see some birds. Maybe there are just a few of them, flying from tree to tree. Or perhaps they're on a long journey.

If you're extra lucky, you might see dozens or even hundreds of birds—a big "V" of geese, or dark clouds of starlings or sparrows. If you're in the tropics, you might see big brown pelicans flying close together or masses of bright pink flamingos.

But there's one thing you won't see, and that's different kinds of birds flying together. For instance, you won't see sparrows or flamingos joining a V of geese.

There's an old saying that "Birds of a feather flock together." Birds somehow know that they are safer when they're all together. And they're right—it's much harder for a hawk or other predator to pick out a single bird from a big group.

· · ● · · · ● · · · ● · · ·

People tend to gather together, too—it's more fun usually, and one person doesn't have to do all the work! These "flocks" of people include clubs, sports teams, churches and, of course, families. Sometimes, all across the country people are reading the same book, watching the same movie, or watching the same sports game, all at the same time. Then, we're part of a really big flock. We like this feeling of belonging.

A kind of cool thing about humans is that we get to choose whether to be alone or to be around a lot of people. We can be part of a "flock"—on a team, in a club, with our friends. We can also choose to be separate sometimes, by reading alone, taking a walk, meditating, drawing a picture, or practicing a musical instrument.

When we have a balance in our life of things that we do separately and things that we do with others, that helps us feel whole. We don't have to choose just one way or the other.

What do **YOU** think?

When are you part of a "flock?"

When are you out on your own, like a hawk or an eagle?

What are the things you like about each way of being?

What are some things you don't like?

4 Persistence

One hot day in July, I went outside to pick some vegetables. On a bare patch of earth near my garden, I noticed something out of the corner of my eye. It was a black-and-yellow striped wasp, moving around on the dry, dusty patch. I was curious. Why would a wasp be on the ground? Shouldn't it be flying around or feeding on something?

I crouched down for a better look. Now I could see that the wasp was moving its front legs over and over again in the same motion, rolling up a tiny ball of earth! Suddenly, the wasp flew off, carrying the little ball with it.

After picking the vegetables, I walked back past that same spot. The wasp was there again, busily working on gathering another tiny ball of earth. This time I watched and followed to see where the wasp flew. It landed on the front of the house. There, on the bricks, was a little mud nest. I watched as the wasp added this new little ball of mud to it.

I have no idea how many balls of mud the wasp had to make to build her nest, but it must have been thousands. What a long, tedious job! Yet the wasp continued and eventually created many nests, for all her eggs. It was something she had to do in order for her young to survive.

· · · ● · · ● · ·· · ● · · ·

There's no way to know if wasps think about the finished nests while they're building them. They are probably doing it simply by instinct. It's different for humans—we can imagine something in the future and look forward to it. We can practice our pitching or batting, music scales, dance moves, math problems—anything— while thinking about how much we're going to improve. When we imagine the end result we want, it makes doing the practice so much easier. It helps us stick with something. Sticking with something is called "persistence," and persistence pays off. When we stick with something, we get better at it!

What do **YOU** think?

What are some things you do that require a lot of work to get better?

What helps you keep from being bored?

What helps you keep from giving up?

. . . .

. . . .

. . . .

. . . .

. . . .

. . . .

. . . .

. . . .

. . . .

. . . .

. . . .

. . . .

Note: The wasp I saw is called a mud-daubcr wasp. If you'd like to see one of these wasps in action, there's a cool video on YouTube that you can watch: https://youtu.be/BWr66LEqav0. The wasp in the video rolls up balls of mud from a wet patch of earth. When mud-dauber wasps can't find mud, they will mix their saliva with dry earth to make the little balls of mud, just like the wasp that I watched.

5 Simplicity

One day last summer, I spent several hours pulling out a huge mass of weeds from under the trees in a corner of my yard. The weeds had grown thick and tall—almost up to my waist.

It was hot, boring work, but there was a surprise waiting for me. As I cleared away the weeds, I uncovered a bird's nest in a low-hanging branch. In the nest were four beautiful, turquoise-colored eggs. I just stood there for a few moments with my mouth hanging open. "Wow!"

As I looked at the nest, I wondered so many things. How do birds know how to pick a good location? How do they know what materials to use and how big to build their nests? How do they build a nest so strong that it won't fall apart in the rain and the wind?

I was also amazed at how simple and small the nest was—only as big as it needed to be.

· · ● · · ● · ▪ · ● · · ·

Many years ago, a man named Henry David Thoreau wondered what it would be like to live more simply. He built himself a tiny house next to a pond a little way from his town. He lived there for over two years. It turns out that Henry David was on to something. He learned that you don't need a lot of things in order to be happy.

When we have a lot of stuff, it can start to take over our lives. We're responsible for all of our things, and being responsible takes time and energy. How many times has your mom or dad told you that you had to clean up your room before you could play with your friends? How often have you spent a ton of time looking for something because it was lost in all your stuff? That's just the kind of thing that Henry David was trying to get away from. He found he could be very happy with less. He had more time to do the things he really wanted to do.

What do **YOU** think?

What are the things you really need in your life?

Do you have time to use and enjoy all the things you already have?

How would your life be different if there weren't so much stuff in it?

. . . .

. . . .

. . . .

. . . .

. . . .

. . . .

. . . .

. . . .

. . . .

. . . .

. . . .

Note: The nest I discovered was a catbird's nest.

6 Looking Ahead

I was seven years old, and my friend Laurie and I were playing in the big, wild space behind her house. All through this open area were clumps of big, beautiful, deep green leaves.

I picked a huge bouquet of them and proudly ran home to present this gift to my mother. But instead of hugging me, my mother grabbed the leaves and tossed them out the door. Then she put me into the bathtub with a bar of soap. What was going on?

I had been so excited by these really cool leaves that I never thought to use my nose as well as my eyes. The "bouquet" I brought home was Skunk Cabbage, and there's a very strong reason why it has that name. Those leaves might have been pretty, but their stinky smell had rubbed off on my hands. I smelled pretty bad—like a skunk!

· · · ● · · · ● · · · ● · · ·

Sometimes, something can look so wonderful that we only see it one way. For instance, we want a new bike or computer game. We want it so much that we can't see that this particular bike isn't built very well and we might get hurt while riding it. Or we can't see that if we get that new computer game, we won't pay enough attention to our homework, music lessons, or even our friends.

Or maybe there's a group of kids we want to hang with—they look like they're having more fun than we are. But we don't really have anything in common with them and we'll never feel comfortable in that group.

Skunk Cabbage teaches us to "follow our nose"—like a detective. It reminds us to take a moment to think about how things "smell" and feel. For instance, imagine what would it really be like if you were part of that group?

Sometimes we have to try things to know about them. Changing our minds later doesn't mean that we were wrong in the beginning.

It just means that now we have better information. If I had stopped to sniff the first skunk cabbage leaf I picked, I might have decided that it wasn't a good idea to pick more!

What do YOU think?

What is a time when you leaped into something because it looked good?

When you got there, was it how you expected it would be?

How might you have made a different decision?

7 Using Your Voice

Yesterday, it rained all day and all night, leaving puddles everywhere. But the heavy spring rain brought something else besides water—it brought the little frogs known as peepers. Late at night I heard them singing in their high, silvery voices from the pond down behind the house.

During most of the year, peepers live in forests and woodlands. In early spring, they hop out of the woods looking for water—ponds or big puddles—where they can mate and deposit their eggs. Then, they go back to the forest until the next spring.

Peepers are tiny frogs, barely an inch long. They are mostly tan, brown, or olive green in color. Their size and their coloring makes them almost impossible to see among the fallen leaves on the forest floor. But their voices are big! The call of a single peeper can be heard all through my neighborhood. When dozens of them are gathered in one pond, they really make a racket. Just ask anyone who has a pond in their backyard.

· · · ● · · · ● · ● · · · ● · · ·

In this big world of ours, it's easy to feel small and unnoticed. There are so many people in our school, in our town, in our country—in the world! It's easy to believe that our one voice won't be heard.

The truth is that one voice can make a difference. One peeper arrives and starts singing at the pond. He lets other frogs know he's there. Soon, more peepers arrive. They join their voices, and the chorus swells. More and more peepers find their way to the pond.

It can be that way for people, too. Sometimes, all it takes is for one person to be courageous enough to speak out. To say, "That's not fair; everyone needs a chance." Or to say, "Don't pollute the water."

Your voice doesn't have to be super loud. You just have to speak up. Sometimes it's hard. And sometimes no one else joins their voice to yours. But you'll feel better knowing that you were true to what you believe.

What do YOU think?

What are some ways that you use your voice?

What does it feel like when you feel heard?

How does it feel when you don't?

8 Discovery through Change

Something exciting happened recently at a large pond a few miles from where I live—a family of beavers moved in! I've never actually seen any of the big rodents, but I've seen the results of their work: three lodges made of branches and lots of tree stumps with "beaver chew" written all over them.

Now, something even more unexpected has happened. At the place where the water of the pond spills over into a little stream, "seashells" have started showing up. The shells are large, about six or seven inches long. They look a lot like clam shells. Where did they come from? It turns out that these are the shells of freshwater mussels, which are related to clams.

Because this kind of mussel lives on the bottom of streams and ponds and because this is a very deep pond, no one had ever seen the mussels there before. It was the beavers digging around on the bottom of the pond as they built their lodges that brought the mussels to light. If the beavers hadn't dug them up, no one would know that the mussels were there.

· · · ● · · · ● · · ● · · · ●

Change is happening all the time. Some changes are so small we barely notice, like grass growing. Other changes are so big we can't possibly ignore them, like when a new baby or a pet arrives at our house.

Some changes are fun, like being old enough to stay up later at night or sleep over at a friend's house. Finally being tall enough to go on the best rides at the amusement park. Making a new friend. Starting a new sport.

Some changes can be a little scary, like moving to a new town and a new school, getting a new teacher, or going to sleep-over camp by ourselves.

The cool thing about change—whether scary or fun—is that just like the beavers in the pond, change often brings new things to light. For instance, at a new school you might find that you now have a chance to be on a sports team they didn't have at your old school. Or, you might meet an amazing new friend.

What do **YOU** think?

Can you remember a change that brought something something interesting or fun into your life? How did you feel about it?

Is there a change that you're worried about right now? If there is, can you imagine that something really cool might happen from it?

9 Being a Leader

If you look up at a "V" of geese flying overhead, you can see that there's one goose who's the leader. It's hard work being the lead goose. The bird out in front at the point of the V has to decide which direction to go. The lead goose also has to cut through the resistance of the air and that gets tiring. The rest of the geese all benefit from the leader's efforts. So from time to time, one of the other birds takes over the lead position. It's like when a coach calls in a relief player in the middle of a game.

How do geese decide when to lead and when to follow? No one knows. But taking turns leading helps the geese keep flying mile after mile on their long migration routes.

· · · • · · · • · · · • · · ·

As a person, what makes a good leader? Do you have to be extra strong or extra smart? Most leaders don't start by thinking, "I want to be a leader." Most people find themselves being leaders because they take actions that other people want to follow. There's a funny scene in the movie *Forrest Gump*. Forrest decides that he's going to run across the whole United States, just because he loves running. When people see what Forrest is doing, they think, "Wow! This guy must know the answers to everything about life. I'm going to follow him!" Before Forrest knows it, he's got a group of people running along behind him. He's like a goose at the head of a V.

This kind of leadership is "leading by example." We do something we believe in, and people may see and join us.

Leadership doesn't have to be running a big company or being the President of the United States. Leadership can be standing up for what you believe is right and fair. Leadership can be lending a helping hand or a friendly smile. You can lead by taking responsibility for yourself and not waiting for your parents to nag you. You can even lead by deciding to be happy.

What do **YOU** think?

What will you do today as a leader?

How does it feel to be out in front?

Is it scary? Exciting? Both?

10 The Power of Stillness

In warm weather, water always seems to be in a hurry. It pours down in rain, runs down street drains, and rushes along in streams and rivers. How different it is when the weather turns cold and water turns to ice! Every winter, I love watching as the pond in our village freezes over. Day by day, as it gets colder and colder, there's more and more ice until finally it covers the whole pond. Now, instead of swimming in the water, the wild geese are standing on top of it!

What life in a pond can possibly survive when it gets this cold? Lots of things! Ice is hard and cold, but it provides protection. That's because ice is lighter than water. As it floats on the surface of a pond or a river, ice insulates the water underneath and keeps it from freezing below.

Deep down in the protected water under the ice, the fish are alive, and the frogs burrowed in the mud at the bottom are alive, and all the tiny little creatures that you can only see with a microscope are alive. That hard, icy covering keeps them safe until warmer weather returns.

· · · ● · · · ● · · · ● · · ·

Ice can remind us that sometimes being still and quiet is helpful. If something is really confusing to us, if our feelings have been hurt, or if we feel really angry, maybe our heart needs some protection.

Maybe you had a fight with your best friend. Or maybe your mom or dad or teacher told you to do something that you didn't think was fair and you got angry. Maybe a pet or a relative died and you felt sad.

When something like that happens, we might not feel like being with our friends or family. We might want to spend a little time alone until our heart settles down and we feel calm again.

You won't always feel like you need to be still and quiet. It's just for a little while. Just like with ice, when the time is right your heart will thaw, too.

What do YOU think?

Has your heart ever felt like it needed some protection?

When are some times that you felt like you needed to be really still and quiet for a while?

Did being still and quiet help you feel better?

11 Steadfastness

Trees don't seem to do much. They stay rooted in the same place for their entire lives and they grow really slowly. Most of the time, we don't pay much attention to them.

The truth is that trees are busy every day, doing things that are very important to us humans. Some of those things are easy to see. For instance, trees provide shade that protects us from the heat of the sun. Think how nice it feels to find a shady spot under a tree on a hot day.

Trees provide lumber for houses, furniture, toys, pianos, and baseball bats. They provide pulp for paper, books, newspapers, and magazines. Trees provide wood for campfires and fireplaces. They provide food: apples, mangoes, almonds, olives, chocolate, and maple syrup. They provide places for animals to build their nests.

Some of what trees do is invisible. For instance, trees produce oxygen—the very oxygen that we and other animals need to live. Under the ground, tree roots hold the soil together.

Trees do all these things by staying right where they are and doing the work that they are designed to do. Nothing much affects them. It can rain or snow. The wind can be calm or blow really hard. The sun can shine or be hidden by clouds. Birds can nest in a tree's branches or fly south for the winter. No matter what the weather, trees keep on providing shade, making oxygen, holding the soil together, and providing homes for wildlife.

· · · ● · · · ● · ▪ · ● · · ·

Maybe that's why many people, for thousands of years, have found strength in trees. They look at trees and think how steadfast they are. "Steadfast" is one of my favorite words. It means holding on tight to a purpose or to something you believe is right. You can think of it as "standing strong."

Being steadfast is not an easy thing. It means holding on to what you stand for. It means keeping your goals in mind. It means sometimes saying "no" to something when it would be easier to say "yes."

What do **YOU** think?

What are some goals you have?

Are you able to be steadfast and work on them, or is it easy to get distracted?

What are some tools you can use to help?

Does it help to let your mom and dad or another trusted adult know what your goals are?

12 Intelligence

If you've been to the beach, you've probably seen empty clam shells washed up on the shore. You may have collected some and brought them home. Maybe you've eaten fried or steamed clams at a restaurant.

Clams don't have arms and legs. They don't move around much at all. They don't have eyes. They don't make any sounds. They're also pretty small, which means that their brains must be pretty tiny, too. So, how smart can a clam be?

Compared to human beings or other obviously intelligent animals such as chimpanzees, dolphins, and parrots, clams aren't smart at all. They can't talk, make tools, or learn to do tricks. But in a certain way, clams are exactly as smart as we are. Clams, like other creatures, have a kind of "innate" intelligence. It doesn't have anything to do with brains. It's just part of being alive.

The soft body of a clam is supported by an external (outside) shell. The clam doesn't have to learn how to make the shell. It's something its body knows how to do automatically: it takes calcium from the sea water and uses it as the building block to make the shell. Calcium is a strong material, so it's a good choice for that.

· · · ● · · · ● · · · ● · · ·

Unlike a clam, our human bodies don't have a hard external shell. We're supported by an internal (inside) skeleton. But, just like a clam, our skeleton is also made of calcium. And just like a clam, we don't have to learn how to make our skeleton. It just happens. Our bodies automatically take calcium from the food we eat and use it to make our bones and teeth. This is why your parents tell you to drink your milk—they want your bones to be healthy and strong, and there's a lot of calcium in milk, yogurt, and cheese. There is also a lot of calcium in some vegetables, and also in some fish, like canned sardines that people eat whole.

What do **YOU** think?

What are some other ways that you're like a clam?

What are some other things your body knows how to do without you doing anything?

· ·

· ·

· ·

· ·

· ·

· ·

· ·

· ·

· ·

· ·

· ·

· ·

· ·

· ·

13 We Are All Connected

It's interesting and fun to explore family roots—who our ancestors were and where they lived. My mother's ancestors were from Switzerland. They left that country to come to America in 1727. That's way before the American Revolution! Before the United States was formed. My father was born in Lithuania. His parents came to America in 1906, when my father was just three years old.

When people compare ancestors and where they came from, it often looks like we're not very connected. "My grandparents came from Ireland." "Mine came from Czechoslovakia." "I'm Chinese." "I'm from India." This looks like a lot of separateness, especially since people from different countries usually speak different languages, eat different foods, and celebrate different holidays. This isn't a bad thing! It's interesting to learn about other countries and different ways of doing things.

· · · ● · · · ● · ▪ · ● · · ·

In looking for ancestors, scientists go further back in history. They search for signs of the very first people on the planet. They look for the answer to the question, "When did humans begin?"

That's a big question, and to find the answer we have to travel back in time. Way back! Back to before there was any life on Earth. Back before there *was* an Earth. Back to when a giant star exploded, spewing out huge clouds of starry stuff. Gradually, the swirling star bits gathered into planets. One of them was our Earth.

Life on Earth was formed out of the building blocks of that star-stuff. Our bodies are made out of the elements of our "ancestor" star; things like calcium, magnesium, iron, carbon, potassium, sodium, sulfur and chlorine. Our bodies are 70% water, and water is a combination of the elements oxygen and hydrogen. And, maybe most importantly, we breathe oxygen—we can't live without it! Even the vitamins we need to be healthy are formed from the different elements.

Remember the clam we talked about yesterday? Remember that a clam's shell and a person's skeleton are both made of calcium? That calcium came from our ancestor star. Go back far enough in Time, and we find that all life on Earth shares a common ancestor. We are all connected!

What do YOU think?

How does thinking about all of this help you feel more connected to the people in your neighborhood, your country, the world?

How does knowing this help you feel more connected to other life on our planet?

14 Preparation

In wintertime, things look pretty dead outside. The trees have lost all their leaves and stand bare against the sky. Nothing is growing

Then spring comes with its gentle rains and warm breezes. The plant world wakes up. There are flowers everywhere—bright crocuses, daffodils, and snowdrops. The trees burst into bloom. The grass turns bright green. Suddenly, like magic, everything is full of color! How do plants do that?

The secret of each year's beautiful, sudden spring is that a lot of it is done the year before.

All during the warm seasons, plants bloom and produce seeds. These are the seeds that will sprout the next spring. Plants also make flower buds and leaf buds in the summer. These buds will stay tightly closed all winter.

When you're outside on a winter day, stop and take a look at a twig on a tree or shrub. The buds you see on the twigs and branches were made last summer. They are just waiting for the warm spring weather to open up and let their flowers and leaves come out.

· · · ● · · · ● · · ▪ · ● · · ·

There are many things that people find helpful to do ahead of time, too. For instance, most people who celebrate Christmas plan their gifts in advance. They know that if they wait too long, they may not be able to find what they want. They might not be able to have the gifts wrapped and waiting under the tree or sent in the mail. If they wait until Christmas Day, they'll find that all the stores are closed. They will have missed the chance to give gifts that year.

There are many other ways to be ready—to have homework, chores, and practicing done—so that when an opportunity comes, you are ready to take it. So that when there's a test or something fun to do with your friends or family, you're prepared.

What do **YOU** think?

What are some of the things you do to be prepared?

Do you ever wait until the last minute?

How does it feel to rush and worry?

Did you ever have to tell a friend you couldn't do something fun because you didn't get your work done ahead of time?

What can you do in the future so that doesn't happen?

15 Optimism

Usually, I take a walk in the morning when I get up. But I woke up earlier than usual today. It was still dark outside, and when I checked the weather report it said it was only 48 degrees. That's not super cold, but my body was still used to warm, summer weather. On this morning, it felt too cold and looked too dark. I didn't want to leave my house!

Finally, I got myself out of bed and put on my walking clothes. Because it was chilly, I added a few extra layers and even my hat and mittens. Then I went outside into the dark. It felt mysterious, like it was the middle of the night.

The darkness didn't last very long. Soon I noticed a brightening in the eastern part of the sky, beyond the hills. The hint of light grew stronger and brighter. And then, suddenly, the sun appeared. As I walked, the big yellow ball of the sun climbed higher in the sky, shining down light everywhere and turning the sky a beautiful blue.

In the growing light, everything became visible. I could see houses, cars, and street signs. I could see trees and grass. As the light grew even brighter, I felt a sort of smile growing inside me. The cold and dark and mysteriousness were gone. I felt happy, and bright like the sunshine. My mood changed completely. I realized that in focusing on the dark, I had forgotten that it would soon be light.

· · · ● · · · ● · · · ● · · ·

You may have heard someone say, "It's always darkest before the dawn." That sounds a little silly. Of course it's darkest in the middle of the night. Everybody knows that! This saying is just a reminder that when things look tough—when we're having a bad day or a bad week—things will get better.

This isn't an excuse to stay in a bad mood. It's important to remember to let the sun come up in your heart and let yourself feel happy again. Sometimes, you can even decide to change your mood.

What do **YOU** think?

If you're feeling bad or sad, does it help to think about something that makes you feel happy?

Would you try it and see? It might take some practice.

16 Being Yourself

There's a wildflower called chicory that grows in places where not much else will survive. I've seen it growing in dry, rocky areas and along roadsides where there's lots of car exhaust and pollution. Chicory doesn't look like much—the stems are scraggly and tough and the leaves are small and pale. The plant just kind of fades into the background.

Most people consider chicory to be a weed and don't give it a second glance. They certainly wouldn't plant it in a garden. But I think chicory is beautiful. I admit that most of the time it's not much to look at. But in the middle of the summer the flowers come out: lovely, purplish-blue flowers with lots of little petals. The blossoms aren't big, bright and showy like roses or sunflowers. But they are quietly beautiful.

· · · ● · · ● · ▪ · ● · · ·

Chicory makes me think about how people are like plants. Both people and plants have personalities. Some people are like sunflowers: they're bold and outgoing, and have a way of naturally standing out—the class president, the star athlete, the homecoming queen.

Some people are like roses: beautiful and talented, but perhaps also shy and tender. They grow "thorns"—bristly personalities that keep others at a distance.

Some people are like herbs, such as peppermint or oregano: they do their own thing, put down deep roots, and you feel good just being around them.

And some people are like chicory: they don't discover their talents right away; they don't like being in the spotlight. But they're also tough, resilient and self-reliant. They don't try to be something that they're not. They're happy with who they are. And they're beautiful that way.

We humans are lucky. We can decide if we want to change how we are. We can be more responsible, more generous, more kind. Deep down, though, each of us has a personality that is all ours, one that we should honor, respect, and be friends with. Each of us is enough, just as we are.

What do **YOU** think?

If you were a plant, what kind of plant would you be?

Do you ever wish you were more like someone else?

How does it feel when you try to be something that you're not?

17 Accepting Change

Have you ever seen a cicada? Cicadas are big, buzzy insects with bulgy eyes and giant, see-through wings. They're creepy to look at, but they're also interesting. To me, the most fascinating part of a cicada is what it leaves behind as it grows.

Cicadas have a kind of bizarre life cycle. Females lay their eggs inside the branches of trees. When the baby cicadas (called "nymphs") hatch out, they drop to the ground. There, they burrow deep into the soil—sometimes 8 feet! They stay safe underground, tunneling and feeding. Some species stay below for 17 years!

When it is time, they dig their way out of the earth and climb up onto the trunk of a tree. Then they shed their skin, wait for their wings to unfold, and finally fly off to live the rest of their lives. The skin stays behind, stuck right onto the tree. The weird thing is that the old, dry skin looks just like a real cicada, as if the creature were still inside it.

· · · ● · · ● · · · ● · · ·

In a way, people are like cicadas. No, we don't ever wriggle out of our skin and leave it behind the way a cicada does. But we leave other things behind as we grow.

Every year you grow taller and bigger. As you grow, you have to leave your small clothes and shoes behind. In school, you leave teachers and books behind. Toys and games you used to like seem boring now. You've moved on to other things. All this is a natural part of growing and growing up.

Sometimes you have to leave things behind that you don't want to. For instance, if your parents move, you have to leave behind your house, your friends, your neighborhood, and your school—things that were familiar to you. This time of change, of leaving things behind, can feel really difficult.

But even when things change, YOU are still there! All of you. You're still you, and you can have a wonderful life wherever you are. The whole point is to grow, and to keep exploring and learning all that you can.

What do **YOU** think?

What are some things you've left behind?

What are some new things you're enjoying?

What are some things you can do when you're bigger?

18 What's Your Signature?

If you get "icked out" easily, you might not want to read this section. But please do anyway. It's not really that gross! Well, maybe it is. It has to do with poo. Animal poo, and what we can learn from it.

Like paw prints or footprints, animal droppings are distinct. They're kind of like a signature. They might say, "An owl was here." Or maybe they say, "A deer was here." Even though you may never actually see the animal, if you find its droppings you know it's been there.

In my garden, I sometimes find droppings of deer and rabbits. That helps me know what's been eating the vegetables in my garden! A few times, I've found raccoon droppings. Once, I found a feathery owl "pellet."

Another word for animal droppings is "scat." Scat can tell researchers a lot about different animals—for instance, what animals are living in a certain area and what they are eating.

· · · ● · · · ● · · · ● · · ·

Every creature leaves something behind. We humans, like all mammals, leave carbon dioxide behind when we breathe. (Mosquitoes use that carbon dioxide to home in on a quick meal!) Birds lose feathers. Porcupines lose quills. We humans shed hair and even our skin cells. Beavers leave behind gnawed tree stumps. Male deer leave behind the velvet from their new antlers each spring. Snakes leave behind their old skin.

People also leave much more behind. Sometimes it's paintings or other works of art they've made. Sometimes it's a world record they set. Sometimes it's a book they've written or a movie they directed. Sometimes it's a new business or product, or a new medicine or way to help people. And sometimes people leave behind a good feeling from being around them—we come away feeling happier or inspired or peaceful.

What do **YOU** think?

What do you "leave behind?"

What could people tell about you from it? For example: do you leave trash and litter behind or do you clean up after yourself? Do you leave angry words and bad feelings behind, or do you practice being kind to others?

Do you think it's important to be careful what you leave behind?

. . . .

. . . .

. . . .

. . . .

. . . .

. . . .

. . . .

. . . .

. . . .

. . . .

. . . .

. . . .

Special Note: Please be careful to never touch animal droppings. They can carry diseases.

37

19 Growing like a Tree

Last summer, a bolt of lightning struck one of the big oak trees in my neighbor's yard. *Crrraaaaack!* The tree split open from top to bottom. My neighbor hired someone to safely remove the broken oak. Down came the branches, limb by limb; then the tall trunk, section by section. Finally, there was just a big stump left.

I was sad that this beautiful tree had been destroyed. But the stump gave me a great opportunity to look at the tree rings.

How do the rings form? During the warm part of the year, trees take energy from the sun and nutrients from the soil. They use this energy and food to grow. As trees grow up, they also grow out, providing a sturdy base for all their branches. Each year this new outward growth shows up as a new ring of wood. I knew that if I took the time to count the rings, I could find out how old the tree was.

· · · ● · · · ● · · · ● · · ·

Like trees, we humans take in energy and grow year by year. Our growth is different, though. We don't add layers onto our outside. From the inside, everything in us grows bigger—our bones, our heart, our lungs, our brain, and even our skin, which contains it all.

A tree's bark is like its skin. The bark has to be tough in order to protect the newly-grown wood just inside. The bark must also be flexible enough to grow and expand as the tree grows and expands.

As I looked at the stump, I realized that a tree is kind of like a loving family. The child is like the heart of the tree, living and growing, getting bigger and stronger. The parents, grandparents, aunts, and uncles are like the tough bark, protecting each new layer of the child's growth. The family must also stay flexible, stretching and expanding so that the child can grow.

What do **YOU** think?

Can you feel yourself growing month by month and year by year?

What are ways that your family holds and protects you—like tree bark?

Does it ever feel that your family "bark" holds you too tightly? Or do you feel you have plenty of room to grow and expand?

....

....

....

....

....

....

....

....

....

....

....

Note: How old was my neighbor's tree? I counted nearly 100 rings!

20 When to Get Involved

One day in May I looked out my window and saw a dark, fuzzy clump moving around in the back yard. When I went outside to take a closer look, the fuzzy clump turned out to be four baby raccoons. They were clumsily climbing over each other, trying to walk, and falling down again in a heap. There was no sign of the mother raccoon, but I figured she must be nearby.

From time to time during the day, I peeked out of the window. The raccoon babies were still there. I started to get worried. Finally, I searched on the internet and found a local wildlife "rehabber." (That's a person who takes care of orphaned or injured wildlife.) She told me that baby raccoons would never leave the nest on their own. Something must have happened to the mother, and the babies had come out to look for her. Out by themselves, they were in danger of starving or being attacked by a hawk. "Can you capture them and bring them in?" she asked.

I called a friend to help me. Together, wearing thick gloves to protect our hands, we gathered up the babies, put them in a cat carrier, and took them to the wildlife rehab center. Several months later the raccoons were released back onto my property. They were big, beautiful, and healthy. It was wonderful to see them again!

· · · ● · · · ● · · ● · · · ●

It's important to learn when helping is truly help, and when help might be harmful. Sometimes animals need to be rescued in order to survive. Sometimes they don't. It's also important to know how to stay safe around wildlife. It's a good idea to ask an expert what to do.

We sometimes see people or friends who look like they're in trouble. Because we have a kind heart, we want to make things better. Some ways to help are easy, like picking up a book someone has dropped, or holding a door open.

But sometimes helping can be unsafe and can even get us into trouble. For instance, suppose a friend hasn't studied and asks if he or she can copy our test paper?

It's hard to accept, but sometimes people need to help themselves.

What do **YOU** think?

Have you ever helped someone and later wished that you hadn't?

What does it feel like to help someone who really needs support?

21 Being in the World

Have you ever seen a butterfly or a moth? Some butterflies are so big and so colorful that it's hard not to notice them. But we don't so often see the butterflies' cousins, the moths. That's because moths only fly at night.

People can be a little like butterflies or moths in their personalities. The "butterflies" are the people we know who always seem to be noticed. They speak up in class. They have lots of friends. They always seem to be doing something bold and exciting.

The "moths" are the people we know who are quieter, who might not like to join groups. They might prefer riding their bike around the neighborhood rather than hanging out at the mall, or would rather read than try out for cheerleading.

Not everyone has to stand out. And standing out or not doesn't make one person better than another. It just means that they're different.

Can you guess which kind of person I am? Like many writers, I'm a little shy. I have ideas I'd like to share, but I'm not very courageous when it comes to talking to a lot of people. I'd rather write down my words and let them speak for themselves. I'd rather go to a quiet gathering with a few friends than to a big party. This doesn't mean that I never go where there are large groups of people. I do!

It's good to challenge ourselves by doing things outside of our comfort zone every now and then. When we face challenges, we give ourselves an opportunity to grow. I'm not talking about things that are dangerous to do, but things that kind of go against our personality a bit. The idea isn't to try and change yourself, but to give yourself different experiences.

For instance, if you always want to be with people, try spending some time alone every now and then. Read something. Draw a picture. Write about how you feel. If you usually like to be alone, try saying "Yes!" to an invitation to do something with a group.

Being able to be in groups and being able to be by yourself are both important skills to have.

What do **YOU** think?

Would you rather spend time by yourself or with your friends?

Do you ever wish you had a different personality?

Do your friends ever tell you they wish they could be more like you?

22 Communicating without Words

One of the things I love to do in the summertime is watch for fireflies. During the day these beetles hang out on the undersides of leaves or on blades of grass. After the sun goes down, they take wing, flashing their tiny lights.

Some of the fireflies stay close to the ground. Others fly high up into the dark canopies of the trees. There, they look like miniature Christmas tree lights. They also remind me of Disney World at night—magical.

What looks magical to us is survival for fireflies. In the darkness, flashing a light is how fireflies communicate. The flashing is part of their mating display. It's how fireflies let each other know that they're there, and helps them find each other.

· · · ● · · · ● · ▪ · ● · · ·

We humans do a lot of communicating with words. We talk to each other when we're together. We talk on the phone. We text. We FaceTime and Skype. We post messages on social media. We send emails. Some of us even write letters by hand. We write books. We publish newspapers, magazines, websites, and blogs. So many words!

But, just like fireflies, we also communicate without using words. For instance, it's easy for your mom or dad to know if you're happy, sad, angry, or confused just by looking at your face.

You might know that a friend doesn't believe a story you're telling them when you see their eyebrows go up. "Really?" their eyebrows say. Our tears can tell others that we're sad and need a hug. Arms crossed on our chest and a scowl can say, "I'm in a really bad mood. Don't bother me!" Red cheeks say, "I'm embarrassed."

A blank stare can tell a teacher that we're bored. A wrinkled forehead can say we don't understand something. Slumped shoulders may say that we're feeling discouraged or shy.

Many times we're not even aware that we're sending out signals and that people are picking up on them.

What do **YOU** think?

What do your unspoken signals tell others about you?

Do you think these make a difference in how people relate to you?

· ·

· ·

· ·

· ·

· ·

· ·

· ·

· ·

· ·

· ·

· ·

· ·

· ·

· ·

23 Letting off Steam

It's usually easy to tell when it's about to rain. Dark clouds move in, blocking out the sun. The air may get very still, or the wind may start to blow in little fits and gusts. It's obvious that something is about to happen.

What's harder to know is what the storm will be like. Will it be a brief, drenching downpour with flashing lightning and booming thunder? Will it be a light, steady rain that falls for hours? Or will the rain fall, stop, and begin again, over and over, all day?

The way that the rain falls can be different at different times. The results can be different, too. In a light, steady rain, there is time for the soil to absorb the water. Rivers and streams can handle the extra water without overflowing their banks. But with a big, heavy downpour, the rain falls so fast that the water runs right off of lawns and pours down streets. Streets can get flooded and creeks rise above their banks. If the winds are strong, branches can break. Whole trees may topple over. Power lines might come down and leave neighborhoods in the dark.

· · · ● · · · ● · · ● · · ·

The feeling of anger is a lot like storm clouds. When we're upset and angry but we haven't told anyone what we're feeling, that's like the dark clouds that gather in the sky. Our family and friends might be able to see that something is bothering us, but it's not in the open yet.

Imagine your anger is like rain stored up in a cloud. Imagine releasing your anger with calm words, like a light, steady rain. Now imagine releasing your anger with lots of yelling, like a thunderstorm. When you let anger build up and then burst out, it's easy to say something that you don't really mean, something that hurts someone else. Your angry words can be damaging like lightning or mighty winds.

It's not always easy to do, but it's usually better if we can let out our angry feelings in a controlled way, without any lightning bolts. We can talk, ask questions, try to forgive. We can avoid damaging our friendships and relationships.

What do YOU think?

Have you ever been in a situation where you got really angry and hurt someone else's feelings, or made them afraid?

How could you avoid that in the future?

. . . .

. . . .

. . . .

. . . .

. . . .

. . . .

. . . .

. . . .

. . . .

. . . .

. . . .

. . . .

24 Seeing Results

Suddenly, right in the middle of my neighbor's beautiful green lawn, there are dozens of bright orange mushrooms. The mushrooms weren't there yesterday. Where did they come from? Did they really spring up overnight?

Most plants grow so slowly that we don't even notice the changes. The only way we can see how it happens is to do time-lapse photography. In this process, someone takes a photo of a plant every hour or every day, and then puts the photos together into a video. When we view the images at high speed, in just a few moments we can watch a tiny seedling grow into a full-sized tree.

··· ● ··· ● ·ₐ· ● ···

Seeing the mushrooms in my neighbor's yard reminded me of the first *Harry Potter* book. When the book was printed, it became an instant success. Both kids and adults everywhere were reading it. Just like the mushrooms that popped up in my neighbor's yard, it looked like the author, J.K. Rowling, had written the book overnight.

The truth is that it took Rowling seven years to write *Harry Potter*—years of thinking, imagining, scribbling down ideas, creating characters, imagining plots, and designing Hogwarts. And twelve publishers rejected the story before one finally said, "Yes!"

That's the way it is with so many great things that people do: we see the end result but not all of the work that went into it. These things look like magic, like they just happened. The truth is, there's a lot of hard work behind these big moments.

Have you ever seen someone in your class get an A on a test that was really hard for you? Did you think that they were just lucky? Or have you ever looked at star athletes and thought, "They're just talented. I could never do that?"

If we just look at results, it's easy to think that something is easy for someone else and impossible for us. The next time you think that someone is "just lucky," take a look "behind the scenes" and find out how much work went into it. Chances are that you can do things that are hard for you, if you're willing to try and to keep on trying.

What do **YOU** think?

What are some of the things that you work really hard on?

Have you ever looked at someone else's success and thought, "I wish that were me?"

What can you do to achieve something you want?

25 Flexibility

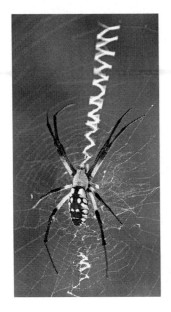

Things have been shaking around here lately! First we had an earthquake. Scary! For about twenty seconds the whole house rocked back and forth as if a giant were shaking it. A few weeks later, we had a hurricane. The wind ripped through the trees and tore off lots of branches, and the rain came pouring down.

When the hurricane was over, I went outside to check on the beautiful black-and-yellow Writing Spider that had spun its zig-zag web next to the house. Surprisingly, the spider seemed completely unfazed by the storm. I found it sitting in the middle of its web as if nothing had happened. The web was perfectly intact.

I was curious: how did the spider survive all that shaking up? Maybe the raindrops slipped right between the strands of the web. Maybe the web was flexible enough to sway in the wind and not be torn apart.

· · • · · • · · • · · ·

Sometimes things in our life shake us up. Someone does something that hurts our feelings. Or maybe our best friend moves away. Or a pet we love dies. When things like that happen, it can feel like there's a storm inside of us—our tears flow down like rain or our anger rages like the fierce wind.

If we try to pretend that we're not hurt or sad, those feelings could get stuck inside us. But if we let ourselves really feel our emotions, even though they're uncomfortable, it's easier to let them go completely. We're free of them.

When I'm really upset, I do things like ride my bike or talk to a good friend. Sometimes I meditate and sometimes I even clean the house! I also write in my journal a lot. My journal is a place where I can say whatever I want about how I'm feeling. And that helps.

What do **YOU** think?

What are some ways that you stay flexible?

What do you do during a "stormy time" when you're feeling bad? I bet that it helps to get hugs from your mom or dad or someone else who loves you.

If you were a spider and could make words on your web, what would you write?

26 The Power of Words

Like gravity, wind is a force that we can feel but cannot touch.

How do we know the wind is there? We feel it on our skin. We hear leaves rustling. We see branches swaying or trees bending over, leaves and litter whirling about. We see ripples on the surface of the water or giant waves crashing on the shore. All this is the work of the wind.

Depending on its speed, wind has the power to help or to harm. A gentle breeze feels good on a warm day. The sound of rustling leaves can calm our spirits. A wind turbine makes electricity as it spins around. But waves can damage the shoreline, move sand dunes, cause erosion, and flood people's homes. The terrible winds of a hurricane can damage houses, knock over trees, and bring down utility poles. Uh-oh! There goes the power!

· · · ● · · · ● · · ● · ● · · ·

This reminds me of the old rhyme, *"Sticks and stones may break my bones, but words will never hurt me."*

I used to think that this was true, that words can't hurt people. But words *can* hurt and they can leave scars, even though they're invisible ones. Mean words can hurt our feelings. Hurt feelings can take a long time to heal. You or someone you know may have already experienced this, either in person or through social media.

In a way, we humans have our own "wind." I'm thinking of the energy that we send out with our words. Our thoughts are like calm, still air: until we speak our thoughts or do something with them, they do neither good nor bad. We might have the kindest thoughts in the world but until we take action for good, nothing happens. A big example in the United States is slavery: until enough people spoke out, slavery continued.

We might have thoughts that aren't very kind toward someone else. If we act on those thoughts, we could be hurtful to the other person. And mean, angry thoughts can actually hurt us, too.

Fortunately, we can choose to not speak those hurtful words. We can choose to not cause harm. And we can even change our thoughts.

What do YOU think?

What are some ways that your words have done good?

What can you say today that might help or inspire someone?

27 Letting Go

Where I live, there are lots of nut trees—oaks, hickories, and black walnuts. I don't really notice them until October, when the nuts start falling. The acorns and the hickory nuts are fairly small. They don't pose much danger. But the walnuts? Yikes! When I walk under the walnut trees I feel like I'm in a game of dodge-ball. The big nuts come hurtling down from high up in the trees. They crash down onto lawns and streets. POW! THUD! SMASH! I don't want them landing on my head!

· · · ● · · · ● · · · ● · · ·

Nature is kind of messy—it's always dropping things! Things like dust, leaves, even pet fur and the hair on our own head.

Most of these things we never notice. Dust falls. We don't see it until it collects on things. A few leaves fall from trees in the summertime. We don't really pay attention until the fall, when all the leaves come down.

When things are no longer useful, nature lets go of them. Most of the time, it's little things like dust, leaves, or hair. Even a walnut falling from a tree isn't a big deal. Losing a tooth can feel like a big event right when it happens. Then our new tooth comes in. We forget about the old one.

Some things are easy to let go of. Some things we hold on to tightly. We hold on to things we know and love: people, pets, even favorite clothes, toys, and stuffed animals. We love our teacher—we want to keep her or him next year. We love our house and neighborhood— we want to stay there forever.

That's good! Wanting to hold on to things shows that we let ourselves connect deeply. It lets us know that we are loving. But being able to let go is important, too.

Letting go of big things that we love can feel scary. Letting go can feel like we're falling. It might help to remember the walnuts.

They can't sprout into a new trees unless they fall to the ground. Letting go is necessary. And there may be a whole different, wonderful life waiting for us when we do!

What do **YOU** think?

What are some things you've had to leave?

What did leaving feel like?

What new things did you find to love?

28 Making Wise Choices

In the little garden right outside my front door, I have
some herb plants—things like mint and basil that I use
in cooking certain recipes. I also have another herb plant
called "rue." I don't use it for anything; I grow it just because
I think the leaves are so pretty.

One morning I discovered twelve small Black Swallowtail
caterpillars (larvae) munching on the leaves of the rue plant.
Obviously, a female butterfly had laid her eggs on that plant,
the eggs had hatched out, and now the larvae from the eggs
were feasting on the leaves. Every day, more leaves disappeared.
Every day, the caterpillars got bigger and fatter. Soon it appeared
that the caterpillars were going to run out of leaves to eat.

I know that swallowtail larvae also feed on dill plants. Dill is an herb
that people use in cooking, so I went to the grocery store and bought
some fresh dill. I hung it on the bare stalks of the rue plant and was
happy to see the caterpillars start eating it right away.

· · · ● · · · ● · ▲ · ● · · ·

Some animals are carnivores—they eat only meat. Caterpillars are
herbivores—they eat plants. Some herbivores, such as deer, can eat
many different kinds of plants. Some, like swallowtail larvae, can
only eat one or two kinds of plants. Even if they're hungry, they can't
eat anything else.

Humans are omnivores. We can eat plants (vegetables, fruits, nuts,
grains), meat (chicken, turkey, beef, lamb, pork), plus fish, eggs,
cheese, and yogurt. We can also eat cookies, chips, soda, French
fries, onion rings, sugary cereal, and candy. How lucky!

Yes, we can eat those things—but should we? "Junk" food certainly
tastes good and it's okay to have it some of the time. But if we eat too
much of the junk, our bodies won't get enough of the vitamins and
minerals we need.

Humans have lots of choices when it comes to food, and that can
make it difficult for us. It's not always easy to make good choices that

keep us healthy. It can take a lot of willpower to say "no" to chips or sweets. Sometimes it's really hard to make good decisions—decisions that keep us healthy and safe today and give us a good future tomorrow.

What do YOU think?

What are some difficult choices you've had to make?

Are there any choices that you think you should change?

Do you think you eat too much junk food?

29 Life, Death, Life

High up on the bank of the creek, at the edge of the road, is a big, old beech tree. I think it's beautiful, but some people might look at this tree and think that it's ugly. They might even think that it should be cut down. That's because the tree is mostly dead. The bark has peeled off in many places and insects have tunneled into the rotting trunk and branches to lay their eggs. Woodpeckers have drilled holes, looking for insects. Different kinds of funguses have started to grow, getting the food they need from the tree itself.

When this beech tree was young and healthy, it was easy to see how beautiful it was. But the tree did much more than provide something nice to look at. Its leaves made shade that cooled the water where the trout like to swim. It produced thousands of nuts each fall that squirrels, chipmunks, birds, deer, raccoons, and other animals could use for food.

Like other trees and green plants, this tree used its leaves to "breathe in" carbon dioxide and "breathe out" oxygen. Oxygen is the most important thing that humans and most other animals need to stay alive.

Truly, this was once a wonderful tree. But even though it's now old, the tree is still useful. At this stage of its life it provides food for insects, which provide food for birds. When the tree fully crumbles away, all the nutrients in it will go back into the soil. Perhaps they will nourish a newly sprouted beech tree, and the cycle of life will continue.

· · · ● · · · ● · · · ● · · ·

Death can be scary—not just for kids, but for adults, too. No one likes to see something get old and die. Whether it's a favorite tree, or a pet, or a grandparent—we feel sad. It feels like the end of something.

But nature shows us that when it comes to life, nothing ever truly dies. It's in a different form, but life goes on. That's the way it's been since the beginning of time, and I expect that's the way it will continue. Part of life is accepting death.

What do **YOU** think?

Have you ever lost something or someone because they grew old?

Is there some part of them that still feels alive to you?

What does it feel like to remember someone or something you lost?

30 Points of View

One thing that most animals have in common is that they have eyes. But not all animals have the same kind of eyes. For instance, among mammals, a cat has eyes that are quite different from a human's; a cat can see much better in the dark than we can. Among birds, a robin's eyes are different from those of an owl or a hawk; robins' eyes help them look out for danger and a hawk can spot its prey from hundreds of feet above the ground.

These different kinds of eyes help the animals survive. Predators have close-set eyes to focus on the animal they're hunting. Prey animals have eyes on the sides of their heads to give them a wider view of any predators approaching. A hawk has eyes that let it see its prey from high up in the sky. A rabbit needs wide vision to see a fox creeping up.

Insect eyes are very different from the eyes of mammals, birds, and fish. Mammal, bird, and fish eyes have just one lens. Most insects have "compound eyes" made up of many separate lenses. For example, houseflies have 4,000 lenses per eye. And dragonflies have as many as 30,000! All those lenses mean that insects don't see shapes very well, but they can easily and quickly detect the slightest motion. Try seeing if you can sneak up on a housefly!

· · · ● · · · ● · · · ● · · ·

As human beings, it's easy to think that each of us sees the same things. But we often don't. For instance, some people see colors very differently from others. What we see also depends on how observant we are, whether we're paying attention to what's around us. Sometimes, even what we're thinking about affects what we notice.

Many arguments begin when a person or group has a certain point of view. They think they're right. But someone else has a completely different viewpoint. They think *they're* right. Neither person or group wants to find out that they're wrong. They hold on to being right as if their life depended on it. Sometimes, these disagreements turn into big conflicts. Sometimes, those conflicts become wars.

There are times when being right or wrong can make the difference between life and death—like whether or not a snake is venomous. But it often happens that being right just isn't important. Many times, it's a matter of opinion, like which flavor of ice cream is the best. The challenge is being able to tell the difference.

What do YOU think?

Can you remember an argument you had with a friend or a parent?

Did it really matter who was right?

Note: When a venomous snake bites, it injects poison into its victim. Depending on the kind of snake, this can be deadly.

31 You, "The Wonderer"

As you've read this book, you've learned about some of my experiences out in nature. You've also seen how it's possible to connect things in the wild world with things in your own life.

Now, I invite you to go out and begin your own observing. Practice noticing what is around you. Look up. Look down. Look all around. Close your eyes and use your ears and your nose. What do you hear? What do you smell?

If you learn how to fully use your senses, you'll find that there is so much to see and to wonder about. The sky's the limit! Or—maybe it's not! There is much to wonder about in space, too.

· · · ● · · · · ● · · · ● · · ·

So, here's my challenge for you...

For one entire week, practice noticing one thing in nature each day and see what you can learn from your observations. It might be something big and grand, like the ocean, or it might be something very small, like an inchworm. Write about what you see and what you think about. You can also draw pictures and take photos. Start your own book!

Note: Yes, you can learn a lot by using your fingers, but you need to be careful. Some plants have sharp thorns or can cause a rash or blisters. Some insects can bite or sting. Unless you are certain that something is absolutely safe, please don't touch it.

What did **YOU** notice?

Pamela Baxter has been exploring the outdoors since she was a child, and throughout her life has instinctively turned to the natural world for inspiration. An educator and a writer, she loves helping others appreciate the beauty and wisdom of nature.

These threads weave together in her professional life. For 24 years she was the editor of the award-winning newsletter of the Valley Forge Audubon Society. She has also contributed articles to the American Horticultural Society's *American Gardener* and to the *Philadelphia Inquirer*. Since 1999 she has been inspiring fellow gardeners through a weekly column in her local newspaper.

As the director of religious education at her church, she loves helping children make deeper meaning of their young lives and their place in the world. A cellist, she teaches privately and performs with a local orchestra and a string quartet.

Pam also enjoys exploring our national parks, hiking, and cooking with the vegetables that come out of her organic garden in Kimberton, Pennsylvania.

You may contact Pam at HiddenOasisPublishing@gmail.com

19439924R00049

Made in the USA
Middletown, DE
05 December 2018